what to eat with what you read

A GUIDE FOR BOOK CLUBS AND OTHER LITERARY GATHERINGS

Suggested menus, recipes, and reading lists from
ROXANE GAY, MIN JIN LEE, ROBIN SLOAN,
MARY ROACH, AND 20 OTHER AUTHORS WE LOVE

**INDEPENDENT
BOOKSTORE DAY**
SATURDAY, APRIL 27, 2019

Table of Contents

Reading Lists

There is no sincerer love than the love of food.

—GEORGE BERNARD SHAW

A River of Stars Vanessa Hua

HAN BAO BAO (ROAST PORK ON STEAMED BUNS) AND LYCHEE MARTINIS

Chinese Roast Pork

2 large onions, thinly sliced

3 garlic cloves, minced

½ teaspoon salt

½ teaspoon pepper

3-pound boneless pork loin roast

¼ cup hot water

¼ cup honey

¼ cup soy sauce

2 tablespoons rice vinegar

1 teaspoon ground ginger

In a slow cooker, combine onions, garlic, salt, and pepper. Set pork on top. Mix together hot water and honey, and stir in soy sauce, vinegar, and spice. Pour over pork. Cook on low for 4 to 5 hours or until meat is tender. Shred pork, and serve on mantou (split Chinese steamed buns). Top with plum sauce (see below) and scallions cut lengthwise.

Plum Sauce

1 pound plums, pitted
   and chopped

¼ cup cider vinegar

¼ cup brown sugar,
   lightly packed

2 tablespoons soy sauce

1 ½ tablespoons grated ginger

1 garlic clove

1 star anise

Combine the plums, vinegar, brown sugar, soy sauce, ginger, garlic, and star anise in a large pot, and bring to a boil. Reduce the heat and simmer until thickened, 20 to 25 minutes. Fish out the star anise and discard. Purée the sauce using a hand blender. Cover, cool, and refrigerate up to 3 weeks.

Lychee Martinis

1 ½ ounces of vodka   Dash of lime juice

1 ½ ounces of lychee syrup
   from canned lychee

Mix the ingredients over ice, stir well, strain, and serve up.
Garnish with a pitted lychee.

What to read next

BROAD STROKES by Bridget Quinn. It's about 15 female
artists from the 17th century to the present. This book is
inspiring, charming, and eye-opening.

FRUIT OF THE DRUNKEN TREE by Ingrid Rojas
Contreras. An enthralling account of female friendship
and girlhood, set in Columbia amid the violence in the
Pablo Escobar era.

ALL YOU CAN EVER KNOW by Nicole Chung. A gorgeous
deeply moving memoir about adoption, the search for
identity, and motherhood.

THE INCENDIARIES by R.O. Kwon. A dark, devastating,
beautiful, inventive, and haunting novel of first love
and faith.

THE GOLDEN STATE by Lydia Kiesling is a lacerating and
lyrical depiction of motherhood.

Part of the secret
of success in life
is to eat what
you like and let
the food fight
it out inside.

—MARK TWAIN

Miss Ex-Yugoslavia: A Memoir
Sofija Stefanovic

WHAT TO EAT
WITH MY BOOK

MY DREAM
DINNER TABLE
The Beatles
and Yoko

RESTOVANI KROMPIR (LENTEN POTATOES), SHOPSKA (BALKAN) SALAD, AND CHICKEN SCHNITZELS

My book is about my immigrant childhood moving between Yugoslavia and Australia. Food from my childhood was always comforting to me and would frequently be cooked by my grandmas. When they visited Australia, they would madly go about looking for ground paprika and Vegeta—two flavors we add to everything, which were hard to find in Australia in the late '80s.

The meal:

Snack on some Smoki puffed peanut treats from a packet (these are well-known in Serbia and available online) while a grandma cooks for you.

Restovani krompir (Lenten potatoes)

6 large potatoes

¼ cup vegetable oil

2 diced onions

Ground paprika to taste

Salt and pepper to taste

1. Peel and dice the potatoes into 1/2-inch squares and parboil them.
2. Heat the vegetable oil on medium heat.
3. Add diced onions to the oil and cook until almost caramelized.
4. Add enough ground paprika to coat the onions.

5. Add the potatoes so that when they are coated in paprika and onion, they turn orange. Taste and add more paprika if needed.

6. Cook until potatoes are soft and mushy.

7. Add salt and pepper to taste.

Serve with:

Shopska salad (mix diced juicy tomatoes, diced cucumber, diced onion, and feta cheese with a dressing of vinegar, oil, and salt) and delicious little chicken schnitzels.

What to read next

THE BEST WE COULD DO by Thi Bui. An excellent illustrated memoir.

THE RED CAR by Marcy Dermansky. A weird and sexy novel about a woman and a haunted car.

IN THE WOODS by Tana French. Scary. Detectives. Dublin.

BRIGHT LINES by Tanwi Nandini Islam. A unique coming-of-age novel set in an ethnically diverse neighborhood in Brooklyn.

Life itself is the proper binge.

—JULIA CHILD

Sourdough: or, Lois and Her Adventures in the Underground Market Robin Sloan

SOUP

It would be easy and also unrealistic to suggest one of the semi-elaborate, quasi-magical dishes from the novel itself, so instead I'll be practical: Eat grilled cheese and tomato soup. Spike the soup with something spicy—a bit of hot sauce or some dried chili flakes. Alternate between bites of grilled cheese and spoonfuls of soup; don't forget to dip. And, at least once, to prove you mean it, drop a spot of tomato soup on one of the book's pages.

Many people have asked me for the recipe for the spicy soup featured in the book's opening pages. I don't have a specific recipe, but I do have some tips that might make any attempt—or any soup, really—more successful:

1. Don't disregard dashi broth. It's easy to make and incredibly flavorful. It also lends a deep umami flavor, so it's a good substitute for meat stocks.

2. Likewise, dried mushrooms can be a magic ingredient! Don't think of them as "mushroom flavor" so much as "instant savoriness."

3. Don't be shy with the spicy. What do you WANT from your soup anyway? Especially in wintertime? You want to feel the hot cleanse. You want to feel (as Lois says in the book) "like a fresh plate, scalded and scraped clean."

Basic dashi broth

4 cup water

2 2-inch pieces of kombu dried kelp

1 cup bonito flakes

1. Warm the water and kombu over medium heat.
2. Remove kombu pieces right before the water reaches a boil (they will be soft).
3. Add bonito flakes, stir and simmer for about 2 minutes.
4. Remove from heat, cover, and let broth steep for 3-5 minutes.
5. Strain bonito flakes from broth.

MOSHI MOSHI by Banana Yoshimoto. This book is anchored in a restaurant and describes as well as anything I've ever read the warmth and melancholy of a favorite haunt. It's about other things, too—family and loss, friendship and death—and all of it is carried along by Yoshimoto's earnest, captivating voice. And, as with any book in translation, it offers an opportunity to get to know the rhythm of a different place and a different language.

CLOSE TO THE MACHINE by Ellen Ullman. The all-time best memoir of programming. But don't think "abstract computer theory"; Ullman's book is sharp, sexy, philosophical, and totally engrossing.

HILD by Nicola Griffith. The ultimate winter book. This one is warm and cozy and totally absorbing, in part because its setting—7th century Britain—is so foreign yet familiar.

EMERGENCY CONTACT by Mary H. K. Choi. Technically YA, but fun and interesting for readers of every age. The book handles text messaging in a fluid, fascinating way; it's simultaneously a master class in narrating the 21st century and a useful look at How the Youth Talk Today.

As long as you're in the food business, why not make sweets?

—ANNE FRANK, *THE DIARY OF A YOUNG GIRL*

The Incendiaries R.O. Kwon

THE PERFECT PICNIC

A picnic like the one Will prepares for Phoebe for one of their early dates. He brings a basket of Stilton cheese, pâté, plum jam, a baguette, peaches, and mulled wine.

Basic mulled wine

2 cups apple cider

1 bottle red wine (something rich like a cabernet or shiraz)

¼ cup honey or maple syrup

2-4 cinnamon sticks

1 orange, zested and juiced (lemons will do too)

4 whole cloves

3 star anise

3 cardamom pods

½ c. brandy, rum, or other liquor (optional)

Combine all ingredients, bring to a brief boil, and then simmer on very low heat until ready to serve. Garnish with orange slices.

What to read next

Lillian Li's **NUMBER ONE CHINESE RESTAURANT**, a wonderfully capacious, insightful, and hilarious novel that would be perfect for a book club.

Notes

Notes

My Year of Rest and Relaxation

Ottessa Moshfegh

A BAGEL

My novel is pretty devoid of meals. The protagonist survives on animal crackers, mostly. She lives on the Upper East Side, and when I imagine walking out of her apartment, I immediately think of a bagel. Not the most exciting meal, but I would suggest eating a whole cinnamon raisin bagel, uncut and untoasted, and drinking some bad coffee with a lot of cream and sugar. This should sustain you. I think it's best to feel a little hungry and dissatisfied while reading my book. If you are full and happy, you might just fall asleep.

I just read and loved **THE MARS ROOM** by Rachel Kushner There's real magic in that novel.

MY DREAM
DINNER TABLE
I'd like James Dean to invite me over for dinner with his best friends. I don't know why James Dean comes to mind. Maybe because I can't really imagine him eating, and certainly can't imagine him cooking. Okay, I can imagine him frying an egg while smoking a cigarette. I'd like to see him follow a recipe for Chicken Kiev, and bake a big chocolate cake, absurd and adorable. Sitting around a table with his friends would probably be more fun than a group I'd put together.

Don't let love interfere with your appetite. It never does with mine.

—ANTHONY TROLLOPE, BARCHESTER TOWERS

Asymmetry Lisa Halliday

WHAT TO EAT
WITH MY BOOK

MY DREAM
DINNER TABLE
Six heretofore
strangers
who are
kind,
curious,
effusive,
hungry,
and
hilarious.
Plus, my
husband.

RED LENTIL SOUP

For reasons of congruity, this dish does not feature on either of the following menus. But the recipe was given to me by the man who inspired the character of Amar. His family would eat it to break the Ramadan fast. It's easy and delicious and accordingly has become one of my favorite staples.

Red Lentil Soup

2 ½ cups dried red lentils (about 1 pound)

1 large yellow onion, minced

2 or 3 cloves of garlic, minced

a generous pour of olive oil

¾ teaspoon ground cumin

1 ½ teaspoons ground coriander

½ teaspoon cayenne

2 teaspoons Aleppo pepper

1 teaspoon turmeric

salt and black pepper

3 ½ cups vegetable broth

cilantro

serrano peppers

1 cucumber

bread

1. Sauté the onions and garlic with the cumin, coriander, cayenne, Aleppo pepper, turmeric, salt, and black pepper.

2. After a minute or two, add the lentils and stir for another couple of minutes.

3. Add the broth, bring to a boil, and lower the heat to simmer.

4. Cook until the soup is reduced to the desired consistency and the lentils are soft.

5. Garnish with fresh cilantro leaves, and serve with serrano peppers, sliced cucumber, and bread.

What you could eat with my book, but probably won't:

Menu #1: "Folly"

Choice of beverage: Ginger ale, Diet Coke, Knob Creek, Sancerre, Pouilly-Fuisse, Luxardo, Champagne

Choice of appetizer: Broccoli with cashews, hacked chicken, Bulgarian caviar, barbecue shrimp, asparagus

Choice of entrée: Spaghetti alle vongole without the vongole, fusilli salsiccia without the salsiccia, salmon, peanut butter with pumpernickel and Tiptree Little Scarlet preserves, hospital chicken

Choice of dessert: Blackout Cookie, praline tart, jelly doughnut, Toy Army Men Gummy Candy

Menu #2: "Madness"

Vending-machine water and a cold curried-chicken sandwich

What to read next

JEFF IN VENICE, DEATH IN VARANASI by Geoff Dyer. A sex- and drug-fueled caper at the Biennale gives way to a darker, moodier, more introspective second half that may or may not represent the first-person consciousness of Jeff in the first half.

Food is an important part of a balanced diet. —FRAN LEBOWITZ

Red Clocks Leni Zumas

WHAT TO EAT
WITH MY BOOK

**MY DREAM
DINNER TABLE**
Sara Ahmed
James Baldwin
Mona Eltahawy
Audre Lorde
Virginia Woolf—
brilliant
thinkers who
are (or were)
unafraid to
speak back
to power,
to question
conventional
wisdom, and
to forge
not always-
comfortable
paths. At a
dinner with
these five,
I suspect
there would
be fierce and
beautiful
arguments.

FAROE ISLANDS MILK-BOILED PUFFIN

This meal includes a favorite food of each main character in *Red Clocks*.

Appetizer: Maize puffs from a vending machine (for the Biographer)

Side: "Ghost pipe," a forest plant that looks like white asparagus (for the Mender)

Entrée: Milk-boiled puffin (for the Polar Explorer)

Dessert: Black licorice nibs (for the Daughter)

Dessert: Pepper-fennel-cardamom chocolate bar (for the Wife)

Milk-boiled puffin (mjólkursoðinn lundi)

1. Skin puffin; rinse.
2. Remove feet and wings; discard. Remove internal organs; set aside for lamb mash.
3. Stuff puffin with raisins and cake dough.
4. Boil in milk and water for one hour, or until juices run clear.

What to read next

THE PACT WE MADE by Layla Al Ammar. A novel about family and secrets set in contemporary Kuwait.

PRETEND WE LIVE HERE by Genevieve Hudson. Dazzling short stories about desire, displacement, queer identity, and Southern Gothic landscapes.

THE CASSANDRA by Sharma Shields. In a suspenseful reinterpretation of the classic Greek myth, a young woman working at a scientific research facility during World War II starts to have terrifying visions of the harm that this research will do.

Notes

Pachinko Min Jin Lee

TAKEOUT KOREAN FOOD

Book club should be about the food. Others may say that it's about the book, and okay, I get it, and as the writer, thank you for thinking about that. However, I love seeing my pals and eating. The reality is that, you don't get to see your book club friends every day, so when you are together, eat well and heartily. Thinking and talking require nourishment.

My kind of book club dinner:

I'd probably order in as much as I could or try to do a potluck so that the host is not overwhelmed. An Asian market like HMart will be helpful if you don't have a decent Korean takeout place available.

Appetizers: mandu or gyoza, roasted salted nuts, and dried cherries. If you can get to an Asian market, go through the snack aisle and have fun. Shrimp chips, rice crackers, wasabi peas, roasted nori …

Entree: Korean fried chicken (I buy mine from Bonchon or Kyochon—I prefer drumsticks). If you have the time or inclination, you can try your hand at making kimchi fried rice. If you can't get to it, buy some gimbop, which is basically rolled sushi, from a restaurant or at a Korean market.

Dessert: I love a big slice of chocolate cake with a heaping serving of vanilla ice cream.

Napa Cabbage Kimchi (paechu kimchi)

This is a kimchi recipe from Momofuku's David Chang. Anything by or inspired by David Chang is wonderful. This recipe makes 1.5 liters.

1 small to medium head Napa cabbage, discolored or loose outer leaves discarded	2 tbsp kosher or coarse sea salt
	½ cup plus 2 tbsp sugar
	20 garlic cloves, minced

20 slices peeled fresh
ginger, minced

½ cup kochukaru
(Korean chili powder)

¼ cup fish sauce

¼ cup usukuchi
(light soy sauce)

2 tsp jarred salted shrimp

½ cup spring onions, coarsely
chopped (greens and whites)

½ cup julienned carrots

1. Cut the cabbage lengthwise in half, then cut the halves crosswise into 2.5 cm-wide pieces. Toss the cabbage with the salt and 2 tbsp of the sugar in a bowl. Let sit overnight in the refrigerator.

2. Combine the garlic, ginger, kochukaru, fish sauce, soy sauce, shrimp, and remaining ½ cup sugar in a large bowl. If it is very thick, add water ⅓ cup at a time until the brine is just thicker than a creamy salad dressing but no longer a sludge. Stir in the spring onions and carrots.

3. Drain the cabbage and add it to the brine. Cover and refrigerate. Though the kimchi will be tasty after 24 hours, it will be better in a week and at its prime in 2 weeks. It will still be good for another couple weeks after that, though it will grow incrementally stronger and funkier.

Reprinted from *Momofuku* by David Chang and Peter Meehan. Copyright © 2009.

What to read next

ALL YOU CAN EVER KNOW by Nicole Chung

HUNGER: A MEMOIR OF (MY) BODY by Roxane Gay

THE MOOR'S ACCOUNT by Laila Lalami

BEL CANTO by Ann Patchett

THE END OF YOUR LIFE BOOK CLUB by Will Schwalbe

THE TWELVE LIVES OF SAMUEL HAWLEY by Hannah Tinti

THE PROFESSOR AND THE MADMAN
by Simon Winchester

Everything you see I owe to spaghetti.

—SOPHIA LOREN

Never Have I Ever
Joshilyn Jackson

MY DREAM
DINNER TABLE
About **15** years
ago, in
Monroeville,
I learned Harper
Lee was at her
Alabama home.
I walked the
streets in a
state of near-
terror, hurling
myself behind
parked cars
and into bushes
every time I saw
an older lady.
All this to say,
I have a horror
of meeting my
heroes. I am
so afraid they
will be human
and flawed.
What if I do
not like them?
Worse, what if
they don't like
me? The idea
of sitting down
with them for
dinner makes
me long for a
plane ticket
out of town
and some
medication.
I would enjoy
my ideal dinner
party more if
the guests were

LIONFISH CEVICHE

Amy Whey, the narrator of *Never Have I Ever*, loves her job as a scuba instructor. I tried research and YouTube videos and interviews, but the underwater scenes felt off. So I learned to dive, and it really changed the book. It also hooked me! Now my husband and I love scuba almost as much as Amy does.

Lionfish Ceviche is the perfect thing to serve with this book. While I was diving all over Florida to scout locations, I saw a lot of them. They are beautiful and dangerous, with a showy halo of spectacular fins that hide venomous spines. They belong in the Indo-Pacific. In the Atlantic, they are an invasive species with no natural predators. They breed fast and threaten the delicate ecosystem of the coral reefs.

Lionfish Ceviche

Note: If you can't get lionfish, you can sub in any sushi-grade, mild, sweet white fish.

1 pound lionfish filets
   cut into cubes

Salt, pepper, and garlic powder
   to taste

1 finely diced small red onion
   (you can sub in scallions
   for a milder version)

1-2 jalapeño peppers,
   seeded and minced

1 bunch cilantro, chopped

Key lime juice (at least 2 cups)

1 large ripe avocado, diced

2 - 3 Roma tomatoes

Cubed fresh mango (optional)

Tabasco (optional)

1. Generously season the fish with salt, pepper, and garlic powder. You can use freshly minced garlic if you prefer.

2. Combine fish, onion, jalapeño, and cilantro in a glass bowl.

3. Add enough Key lime juice (fresh squeezed is best!) to cover the fish entirely, and then place in the fridge for 1 - 2 hours.

4. Remove from fridge and add the avocado, stirring to coat the cubes in lime juice.

5. Drain, add the diced tomatoes. For a sweeter, more tropical taste, you can sub in diced mango for the tomatoes. If the jalapeño isn't doing it for you, you can heat it up with a dash of Tabasco.

6. Serve cold by itself, or over a bed of greens, or with corn chips. It pairs nicely with margaritas, citrus-infused beer, and crisp white wine, but I enjoy it best with gin and tonic. And for this book? You'll definitely want to serve those G&Ts with a twist.

What to read next

I hope you will choose **NEVER HAVE I EVER**. It's perfect for book clubs—it even begins at one. Amy is hosting her neighborhood club when a new woman shows up. Roux is sophisticated and beguiling, with expensive clothes and an even more expensive face. It's a twisty and diabolically entertaining tale of betrayal, deception, temptation, and love.

I'm in two book clubs myself, one that reads chewy but fun contemporary books and another that reads classic literature. Here are my favorite recent reads from each:

FURIOUSLY HAPPY by Jenny Lawson. It's a funny, sharp memoir about not just living, but living well with mental illness. It can open up great discussions about empathy and navigating invisible challenges.

The classics club bent one of our own rules to delve into Octavia Butler's **KINDRED**. It's the story of a modern, young black woman who finds herself pulled back in time to the Antebellum South—deep into her own family history. Blunt, brilliant, suspenseful, and compulsively readable,

purely fictional: Elizabeth Bennet from *Pride and Prejudice* for lively conversation. If it was potluck, I'd invite Bobby Banks and Alice Stone, from Susan Rebecca White's *A Place at the Table*. Bobby was based on real-life celebrity chef Scott Peacock, and Alice on Edna Lewis, the undisputed Grand Dame of Southern cooking. Hopefully, they'd show up with some righteously fried chicken and a huge corn pudding. Hermione Granger from the Potterverse for a little magic and because I flat love Hermione Granger. Last and largest, Lee Child's Jack Reacher. If our dinner party was beset upon by brigands, he'd beat them to pulps and then calmly ask for a little more coffee.

Novels for food lovers

- **Number One Chinese Restaurant: A Novel** by Lillian Li
- **The Hundred-Foot Journey** by Richard C. Morais
- **Sweetbitter: A Novel** by Stephanie Danler
- **Tomorrow There Will Be Apricots** by Jessica Soffer
- **Five Quarters of the Orange** by Joanne Harris
- **Gourmet Rhapsody** by Muriel Barbery
- **The Particular Sadness of Lemon Cake** by Aimee Bender
- **Chef: A Novel** by Jaspreet Singh
- **Delicious!** by Ruth Reichl
- **Kitchens of the Great Midwest** by J. Ryan Stradal
- **In the Kitchen: A Novel** by Monica Ali
- **The Abundance: A Novel** by Amit Majmudar
- **Chocolat** by Joanne Harris
- **Babette's Feast** by Karen Blixen
- **The Whole World Over** by Julia Glass
-
-
-
-
-
-
-
-
-

Notes

The Bucket List Georgia Clark

**WHAT TO EAT
WITH MY BOOK**

CHEESY PASTA

**MY DREAM
DINNER TABLE**
Clara Bow:
Controversial
and
misunderstood,
Clara was a
silent film star
in the 1920s and
America's first
sex symbol.

Michelle
Obama: Tell me
everything,
Michelle. Tell
me everything.

Jane Austen: To
lead the clever
banter and tell
us about life in
corsets.

Freddie
Mercury:
Because Queen.

Kristen Stewart:
For eye candy
and mumbles.
Swoons.

"I'm being so bad." I help myself to a second serving of delicious cheesy pasta. "This is so bad."

"No, this is Saturday night." Steph tucks her feet underneath her, cozying into the couch. Outside, rain rattles the window.

"I remember." I lick my fork. "Living with you was terrible for my beach bod."

"Lace, every bod is a beach bod."

Lacey's best friend Steph is rarely seen without a bowl of cheesy pasta, which also happens to be my favorite thing to eat! There are a million ways to satisfy a carb-related craving, but I like to make Annie's Organic Mac and Cheese, and add in sautéed onion, tomato, and mushroom, and top with extra cheese. A good pinch of Maldon sea salt and plenty of cracked black pepper completes this delicious meal.

What to read next

IN COLD BLOOD by Truman Capote. This was the first book my book club ever did, and it remains one of our best. There is so much going on here: it's a true crime story and portrait of the killers, equally suspenseful and, strangely, empathetic, even beautiful. It's also about the genre of true crime itself (Capote called it creative nonfiction, and it was one of the first of its kind). Our club made food inspired by the book, and even years later, I remember the taste of orange blossom cocktails.

POSTCARDS FROM THE EDGE by Carrie Fisher. I love an acerbic female narrator, and Suzanne Vale will not disappoint. Penned by the great talent that was Carrie Fisher, exposing subjects she knew all too well: addiction, fame, sex, money, and love.

GLAMORAMA by Bret Easton Ellis. This brutal, startling novel is Mr. Ellis in full control of his astounding literary ability. Achingly hip, intensely vacuous Victor Ward accepts a mysterious offer to track down a college friend, Jamie Fields. This plan quickly goes awry, and Victor's shallow life of parties, paparazzi, and posing nosedives into something much more serious and threatening. This very funny, very dark novel elevated my understanding of structure, satire, and the art of story.

ELEANOR OLIPHANT IS COMPLETELY FINE by Gail Honeyman. Eleanor Oliphant is a socially inept loner with no friends, no career prospects, no relationship... and she is completely fine, thank you very much. Or so she thinks. This first-person coming-of-age invites you into the head of the extremely particular Eleanor, in a hopeful tale that cleverly straddles the genres of suspense and romance.

THE REGULARS by Georgia Clark. Hey, that's me! Best friends Evie, Krista, and Willow are just trying to make it through their mid-20s in New York. Until they come across Pretty, a magic tincture that makes them, well... gorgeous. Like, supermodel gorgeous. And it's certainly not their fault if the sudden gift of beauty causes unexpected doors to open for them. But there's a dark side to Pretty, too, and as the gloss fades, there's just one question left: What would you sacrifice to be Pretty?

If more of us valued food and cheer and song above hoarded gold, it would be a merrier world.

—J.R.R. TOLKIEN

Noir: A Novel Christopher Moore

**WHAT TO EAT
WITH MY BOOK**

A CLASSIC SAN FRANCISCO MEAL

**MY DREAM
DINNER TABLE**
Raymond
Chandler.
There was
nobody better
at putting
together a
tough guy
metaphor.

Dashiell
Hammett was
a creature of
San Francisco,
someone who
had really
worked as a
detective.

James M. Cain.
A true master
of character
and the human
heart.

Jim Thompson
was the
darkest of
dark. He wrote
truly morally
ambiguous
stories.

Herb Caen was
the man in San
Francisco. He
knew every
subculture,
every street,
every politician,
and every cop,
and he wrote
about them
with great
affection and
aggravation.

Hors d'oeuvres: Sourdough rounds with crab dip would work very well with a San Francisco setting. However, we also have a great Chinese, Italian, and Mexican culinary tradition, so you can pull out the stops from potstickers to mini tacos to an antipasto tray.

Dinner: Well, a 1940s tough guy dinner is going to be steak, rare, a baked potato or, since it's San Francisco, maybe some penne with parmesan. Clam chowder to start, a big basket of sourdough, and some creamed spinach. Oh yeah, some brown liquor, because it's noir, and there's always brown liquor, although the characters in my book put away a lot of gimlets, which are gin, sugar, and lime juice, or gin and Rose's lime juice. If you're not eating red meat, some snapper, rockfish, or a halibut will do. Dungeness crab is a luxury and can be tough to get, but it's very San Francisco. You could just go with classic diner food, too, of which a lot gets consumed in the book, and maybe a shot of "Old Tennis Shoes," whiskey poured into your Coke under the table.

What to read now

THE AKASHIC NOIR series is just terrific. Gathered by city, from Akashic to Nairobi to Tampa, I think there are over 100 volumes in all. Local authors, both contemporary and classic, are gathered in the collections. For me, true noir (not "perky noir," like my book) can get a little oppressive, so having it in short stories allows you to take a breath now and then. Plus, you get to explore the dark underworld all over the world.

Notes

Notes

The Answers Catherine Lacey

FATTY TUNA SASHIMI—OR NOTHING AT ALL

This is a book about the impossible and irresistible human inclination to reach total perfection and certainty, so whatever you eat it should be fastidiously prepared and plated in such a way to render all your guests speechless—almost shamefully so. *The Answers'* primary narrator, Mary, is ill for most of the book and generally has a hard time eating anything, but her only friend does manage to feed her some pepita paste. So if you're vegan you could go that route: a quiet, lonely meal of organic, sprouted pepita paste while wondering what is wrong with your body. If you're not vegan, you could have an almost prohibitively expensive plate of fatty tuna sashimi, and for dessert you punch someone in the face, as The Anger Girlfriend does. It's your choice. This is a novel of extremes. Good luck.

What is reading

JEAN RHYS: LIFE AND WORK by Carole Angier

OTHER PEOPLE'S HOUSES by Lore Segal

I AM THE BROTHER OF XX by Fleur Jaeggy

BELLY UP by Rita Bullwinkel

CHALK: THE ART AND ERASURE OF CY TWOMBLY
by Joshua Rivkin

MY DREAM DINNER TABLE
What I like the most about dinner parties is when they take unexpected turns. The most esteemed guest starts passing a blunt around, or a good-natured argument breaks out, or someone receives shocking news. I'd invite some people who haven't always behaved very well: Susan Sontag, Charlie Chaplin, Emma Goldman, Igor Stravinsky, and Tsuguharu Foujita. I would ask my partner to make us a tagine, with a lot of preserved lemon.

And believe
me, a good
piece of
chicken can
make anybody
believe in
the existence
of God.

—SHERMAN ALEXIE,
THE ABSOLUTELY TRUE DIARY OF A PART-TIME INDIAN

Girl Waits with Gun

Amy Stewart

**WHAT TO EAT
WITH MY BOOK**

**MY DREAM
DINNER TABLE**
The real people
my characters
are based on:
Constance,
Norma, and
Fleurette Kopp.
I wonder every
day about their
real lives and
what they'd
make of the
stories I've
invented about
them. I'd also
invite Alice
Stebbin Wells,
a pioneering
woman in law
enforcement at
the LAPD who
founded the
International
Policewomen's
Association.
Finally, I'd invite
Mary Roberts
Rinehart, a
bestselling
author of crime
fiction at the
time, in the
hopes that
she'd write a
story about
our dinner
together for
the *Saturday
Evening Post.*

KRAUTFLECKERL

In *Girl Waits with Gun*, Norma's favorite dish comes from Austria, her mother's homeland. It's called Krautfleckerl, and it's made of nothing but cabbage, pasta, onions, and a few spices. But you can elevate this into a delightful, rich, crowd-pleasing casserole by adding bacon, fancy cheese, bread crumbs—you get the idea.

A Kopp sisters' family meal would consist of plain, homemade food like Krautfleckerl, but it would be greatly enhanced by a dessert that they did not have to cook themselves. Their sister-in-law, Bessie, is always popping in with apple pies, upside-down cakes, meringues, and fruit compotes. Add any dessert you like, as long as someone else went to the trouble of actually baking it!

Krautfleckerl (my enhancements in parentheses)

1 large head green cabbage (or what about shredded Brussels sprouts?)

1 onion or leek, chopped (I also add lots of garlic)

3 tablespoons vegetable or olive oil, or more as needed (butter, anyone?)

16 oz package of your favorite noodle or pasta

Salt, black pepper, and caraway seeds

Optional: Top with bacon or sausage, your favorite cheese, bread crumbs, etc.

Preheat oven to 400 degrees.

1. Dice the cabbage or Brussels sprouts into small pieces. Salt lightly and let stand for about 15 minutes.

2. Caramelize the chopped onion in olive oil or butter for about 15 minutes, then add the cabbage and the caraway seeds. Cover and cook, stirring regularly, until light brown in color. Season with salt and pepper.

3. Boil the noodles, drain, and combine with the cabbage mixture. If you're adding optional toppings, pour the mixture into a pan, add toppings, and bake until browned on top, usually 15-20 minutes.

What to read next

THE TRIALS OF NINA MCCALL: SEX, SURVEILLANCE, AND THE DECADES-LONG GOVERNMENT PLAN TO IMPRISON "PROMISCUOUS" WOMEN by Scott Stern. A nonfiction book that reads like a novel and covers the astonishing history of women being jailed for so-called morality crimes, much like what occurred in Constance's time as deputy sheriff.

THE ARRANGEMENT by Ashley Warlick. If you like novels based on real women, try this one about the food writer M.F.K. Fisher and the affair she had with her husband's friend. It's beautifully written, sexy, tragic, and filled with food, Paris, love, tears, and laughter.

I CAPTURE THE CASTLE by Dodie Smith. How about an almost 100-year-old novel about two sisters living in a moldering castle in England under difficult circumstances, in which one is a writer? This novel in diary form, written by the author of *101 Dalmatians*, made me feel the way I felt when I was 10 and I read *The Secret Garden* for the first time.

THE GOLDEN STATE by Lydia Kiesling is a lacerating and lyrical depiction of motherhood.

I am not
a glutton.
I am an
explorer
of food.

—ERMA BOMBECK

Novels with recipes

- **Heartburn** by Nora Ephron
- **Like Water for Chocolate** by Laura Esquivel
- **Big Night: A Novel with Recipes** by Joseph Tropiano
- **World of Pies** by Karen Stolz
- **The Cuttlefish** by Maryline Desbiolles
- **Pomegranate Soup: A Novel** by Marsha Mehran
- **The Debt to Pleasure** by John Lanchester
- **Red Sparrow** by Jason Matthews
- **The Hindi-Bindi Club** by Monica Pradhan
- **Eat Cake** by Jeanne Ray
-
-
-
-
-
-
-
-
-
-
-
-
-
-

White Houses Amy Bloom

POWER AND PRIVILEGE DEVILED EGGS

WHAT TO EAT
WITH MY BOOK

MY DREAM
DINNER TABLE
Well, dinner is
different than
a lifetime or
a love affair.
I don't wish to
offend anyone
living, and
I know the
Obamas are
pretty busy,
so ...

James Baldwin

Robertson
Davies

Octavia Butler

Oscar Wilde
(one-drink limit)

and Colette
(irresistible
in her
dreadfulness)

Eleanor was a lousy cook and not much fun to dine with; she preferred an absence of vice to an abundance of pleasure. Hick, on the other hand, knew her way around a table. Having come from a worse-than-dirt-poor background, she appreciated all things delicious, whether plain or fancy. I'd suggest finger food (because you don't want to spill soup on the book [editor's note: see page TK) a strong cocktail (Sidecars were a favorite, or Old-Fashioneds), accompanied by classic '30s cocktail foods: pigs in a blanket, devilled eggs, cheese straws, Belgian endive spears stuffed with curried crab salad, and Charleston cheese crackers.

Power and Privilege Deviled Eggs

12 eggs

¼ cup mayo

2 t. yellow mustard

2 t. Dijon mustard

2 t. pickle juice

salt and pepper

dash of hot sauce
(I like Frank's hot sauce or Huy Fong's sriracha)

paprika to sprinkle

crumbled crisp bacon

Boil eggs. Shell them. Slice in half and scoop out and then mash yolks. Mix all except the last two ingredients. Slap a dollop into each egg-while half. Top with paprika and bacon. If you maintain a discreet silence, 4 people could easily polish these off.

What to read next

THE DEPTFORD TRILOGY by Robertson Davies

THE STONE DIARIES by Carol Shields

And, of course, my previous novels: **LOVE INVENTS US, AWAY**, and **LUCKY US**

After a full belly all is poetry.

—FRANK MCCOURT

Hunger:
A Memoir of (My) Body
Roxane Gay

WHAT TO EAT
WITH MY BOOK

MY DREAM
DINNER TABLE
Edith Wharton
Beyoncé
Michelle Obama
Sarah Silverman
and my person

A STEAK DINNER

Thick ribeye steaks, grilled medium rare, sautéed mushrooms and onions, crisp green beans, hash browns, a cold Caesar salad, Pinot Noir flowing freely, the satisfaction of satiation.

Steakhouse Steaks

This recipe from Ina Garten works with most any cut of beef.

4 (2-inch-thick) filets mignons, tied (10 ounces each)

2 tablespoons vegetable oil

2 tablespoons fine fleur de sel

2 tablespoons coarsely cracked black peppercorns

4 tablespoons (1/2 stick) unsalted butter, at room temperature

Preheat the oven to 400 degrees.

1. Heat a large cast-iron skillet over high heat for 5 to 7 minutes.

2. Meanwhile, pat dry the filets mignons with paper towels. Brush the filets lightly all over with the oil. Combine the fleur de sel and cracked pepper on a plate and roll the filets on all sides in the mixture, pressing lightly to help the salt and pepper adhere. The steaks should be evenly coated with the salt and pepper.

3. When the pan is extremely hot, add the steaks and sear evenly on all sides (top, bottom, and sides) for about 2 minutes per side. (Be sure the cooking area is well ventilated.) You'll probably need about 3 turns to sear the sides and about 10 minutes total.

4. Remove the pan from the heat and arrange all the filets flat in the pan. Top each with a tablespoon of butter, then place the pan in the oven. Cook the filets for 8 to 12 minutes to 120 degrees for rare and 125 degrees for medium-rare. Remove the steaks to a platter, cover tightly with aluminum foil, and allow at rest for 5 to 10 minutes.

What to read Next

ALL THE NAMES THEY USED FOR FOR GOD
by Anjali Sachdeva

HEAVY by Kiese Laymon

FRAIL SISTER by Karen Green

WHEN I GROW UP I WANT TO BE A LIST OF FURTHER POSSIBILITIES by Chen Chen

MEET BEHIND MARS by Renee Simms

I have made a lot of mistakes falling in love, and regretted most of them, but never the potatoes that went with them.

—NORA EPHRON

Beautiful Ruins Jess Walter

SPAGHETTI CARBONARA

MY DREAM
DINNER TABLE
These dream
dinners
typically
stipulate that
I may choose
anyone "living
or dead,"
but I always
suspected
it would be
awkward dining
with dead
people, given
the cessation
of human
consciousness
and the social
limitations of
decomposition.
And while I
suppose this
would mean
more for me
to eat, I would
also have
to carry the
burden of the
conversation.
So, I will go
with a table of
living reclusive
writers—Elena
Ferrante, Don
DeLillo, Cormac
McCarthy,
Thomas
Pynchon.

My favorite version of this dish is my wife's family specialty, and while I would love to share the actual recipe, it would be a stretch to think a) that it is ever made the same way twice, b) that if there were a "recipe," her family would trust me with it, and c) that if I did share it, I would ever get to eat it again. Suffice to say that's it's spaghetti with pan-fried pancetta, salt and pepper, and maybe some pecorino or parmesan cheese, and, with the spaghetti steaming hot, eggs are cracked and stirred in—the heat from the pasta cooking the eggs as they coat the whole thing. If you're vegetarian, you could go with cacio e pepe (literally, cheese and pepper on pasta). Add some good bread, a great glass of wine, and honestly, I'm not sure you even need my book.

Spaghetti Carbonara (NOT Jess' wife's actual recipe)

2 eggs

3 ounces parmesan cheese

½ cup loosely packed
   flat-leaf parsley leaves

¼ teaspoon freshly ground black
   pepper, plus more for garnish

¼ pound pancetta or thin-cut
   bacon (vegetarians can

leave this out and it will still
be tasty)

2 cloves garlic

3 tablespoons olive oil

½ cup dry white wine

1 tablespoon salt

1 pound spaghetti (good with
   whole wheat pasta, too)

1. Put a large pot of water on to boil. Meanwhile, crack eggs into a large bowl and beat lightly. Finely shred or grate cheese, add ½ cup to eggs, and set the rest aside. Finely chop parsley and add to eggs. Add pepper and whisk to combine well. Set aside.

2. Cut pancetta or bacon into ¼-inch thick slices, peel and chop garlic, and set both aside. Heat olive oil in a small frying pan over medium-high heat. Add pancetta and cook, stirring

occasionally until it starts to brown. Add garlic and cook while stirring, until fragrant, about 1 minute. Add wine and cook until liquid is reduced by about half. Remove from heat and set aside.

3. When water boils, add salt and spaghetti. Boil pasta until it is tender. Drain well and immediately pour pasta into bowl with egg mixture. Toss to thoroughly coat pasta with egg mixture (the heat from the pasta will partially cook the egg and melt the cheese). Pour pancetta mixture on top of pasta and toss to combine thoroughly. Sprinkle with remaining cheese and pepper to taste. Serve immediately.

Makes 4-6 servings

What to read next

A writer I think everyone should know is Percival Everett. He is a wildly protean talent, so you could choose any of his diverse books, but if you want to shake up your book club with a challenging conversation, read **ERASURE**.

Food-centered memoirs

- **Kitchen Confidential** by Anthony Bourdain
- **Blood, Bones & Butter: The Inadvertent Education of a Reluctant Chef** by Gabrielle Hamilton
- **The Art of Eating** by M.F.K. Fisher
- **Heat** by Bill Buford
- **Climbing the Mango Trees** by Madhur Jaffrey
- **Tender at the Bone** by Ruth Reichl
- **The Man Who Ate Everything** by Jeffrey Steingarten
- **My Life in France** by Julia Child
- **Julie & Julia** by Julie Powell
- **A Tiger in the Kitchen** by Cheryl Lu-Lien Tan
- **Animal, Vegetable, Miracle** by Barbara Kingsolver
- **Born Round** by Frank Bruni
- **Home Cooking** by Laurie Colwin
- **The Raw and the Cooked** by Jim Harrison
- **Yes, Chef** by Marcus Samuelsson
- **The Gastronomy of Marriage** by Michelle Maisto
- **My Kitchen Wars** by Betty Fussell
- **The Fortune Cookie Chronicles** by Jennifer 8. Lee
- **Delights and Prejudices** by James Beard
- **My Soul Looks Back** by Jessica B. Harris
- **Never Eat Your Heart Out** by Judith Moore
- **I'll Have What She's Having: My Adventures in Celebrity Dieting** by Rebecca Harrington
- **Cooking for Mr. Latte** by Amanda Hesser

Notes

Is food a
substitute
for love?
No, love is a
substitute for
food. And a
pretty poor
substitute
at that.

—ROHAN CANDAPPA

The Oysterville Sewing Circle

Susan Wiggs

WHAT TO EAT
WITH MY BOOK

OYSTERS, OYSTER CRACKERS, AND THE CAKE OF A THOUSAND FACES

MY DREAM
DINNER TABLE
Madame Bovary
and Juliet
Capulet,
whom we'll
convince to
make better
choices.
Margaret
Dashwood
from Sense
and Sensibility,
because
she'll be the
one to convince
them! Katniss
Everdeen from
The Hunger
Games, will give
us lessons in
self-defense
and survival.
And finally,
Eleanor
Oliphant,
because
she's so
lovable, and
we will show
her the
kindness she
deserves.

Well, oysters are obviously what you should eat, but since oysters are controversial ("He was a bold man that first ate an oyster" —Jonathan Swift) and tricky to prepare, there are other options. Instead, let's do oyster CRACKERS. These are curiously addictive.

Ranch Dill Oyster Crackers

1 (1 ounce) package ranch-style dressing mix

½ teaspoon dried dill weed

¼ cup vegetable oil

½ teaspoon lemon pepper (optional)

¼ teaspoon garlic powder (optional)

5 cups oyster crackers

1. Preheat oven to 300 degrees F (120 degrees C).

2. In a large bowl, combine the dressing mix, dill weed, vegetable oil, lemon pepper, and garlic powder. Add oyster crackers and toss to coat.

3. Spread evenly on parchment-lined baking sheets.

4. Bake for 10 minutes, give everything a stir, then bake another 10 minutes. Cool before serving.

The Cake of a Thousand Faces

This is my standby cake. There's no way to mess up this cake.

1 stick butter (never margarine)

1 cup flour

1 cup sugar

1 tsp baking powder

2 large eggs

1. Beat together all above ingredients.
2. Spread the thick batter into a buttered tart pan.
3. Now add what you want: blackberries pressed into the top of the tart, thinly sliced very ripe pears, raspberries, blueberries, plums, and peaches. Almond flavoring and sliced almonds are good, too.
4. Bake at 350 degrees. Depending on the size of your tart pan, it can take anywhere from 45 to 55 minutes.
5. When cake comes out of the oven, brush with melted apricot jam to make a glaze, or dust with powdered sugar if you'd like and serve with whipped cream.

What to read next

FIRST, WE MAKE THE BEAST BEAUTIFUL by Sarah Wilson. One of those rare books I bought solely for the cover and ended up loving. It's a memoir about dealing with anxiety, but ends up being discussable on many levels.

A SPARK OF LIGHT by Jodi Picoult. It's a great example of entertaining, page-turning fiction that also makes important points about one of the most divisive issues of our time: reproductive rights. So many points of view are dramatized in this novel—perfect for lively discussions.

THIS IS HOW IT ALWAYS IS by Laurie Frankel, a Seattle writer and friend of mine, A book I wish everyone would read—without preconceived notions, without judgment, with an open mind and open heart.

LOVE AND TROUBLE by Claire Dederer. Another friend who lives here on Bainbridge Island has drawn back the curtain on the inner life of women of a certain age. She's damn funny, too.

The Islanders Meg Mitchell Moore

NEW ENGLAND CLASSICS AND WHOOPIE PIE

MY DREAM
DINNER TABLE
Michelle Obama
for wisdom,
glamour and
stories. Dame
Judi Dench for
elegance, wit,
and the glorious
accent. Stephen
King, for writing
advice and that
special Maine
kind of humor.
Julia Louis-
Dreyfus for
laughs! And
more laughs!
And stories
about VEEP!
And my
maternal
grandmother,
Margaret
(Dugan) Harton
(I am named
after her and
never got to
meet her. I
am so curious
about her.)

Appetizer: clam chowder, in homage to the fresh clams from Block Island.

Main course: baked Atlantic cod with lemon and dill, lobster mashed potatoes, and tomato, peach, and burrata salad.

For dessert: a plate of delectable whoopie pies.

To drink: Strawberry ginger mojito followed by a glass (or two) of sauvignon blanc.

Chocolate Whoopie Pie with Creamy Vanilla Buttercream Filling

½ cup (1 stick) unsalted butter, softened

1 cup dark brown sugar

1 tsp vanilla extract

1 large egg

2 cups all-purpose flour

½ cup Dutch process chocolate

1 ¼ tsp baking soda

1 cup buttermilk

Pinch of salt

1. Preheat oven to 375 degrees F (190 degrees C). Line 3-4 large baking sheets with parchment paper.

2. Place the butter, sugar, and vanilla extract in large bowl and beat together until light and fluffy.

3. Sift flour, cocoa, baking soda, and salt into the bowl and mix together.

4. Add buttermilk and stir until combined.

5. Using a level 2-inch/5-cm ice cream scoop or heaping table-spoons, make 24 halves. They will vary in size.

6. Leave at least 3 inches /7.5 cm of space between each one

7. Bake in oven 10-12 minutes until firm to the touch. Transfer to a wire rack to cool.

Creamy Vanilla Buttercream Filling

¾ cup (1 ½ sticks) butter, unsalted, softened

¾ tsp vanilla extract

3 ½ cups confectioners' sugar

1 tbsp milk or cream

1. Place butter and vanilla extract in a large bowl and beat together with a wooden spoon (or electric mixer on low speed) until combined.

2. Sift in the confectioners' sugar. Add the milk or cream and beat together until light and fluffy. Use immediately or store in refrigerator.

3. Take two cooled whoopie pie lids of about the same size and place flat side up. Using a small ice cream scoop, place a scoop of vanilla filling on one lid. Place the lids together gently, being careful not to press too hard.

Makes enough for 12 whoopie pies

Adapted from the award-winning Chococoa Baking Company recipe.
Copyright © 2014 Chococoa Baking Company, Inc. All rights reserved.

BEARTOWN by Fredrik Backman. I was a little late jumping on the Fredrik Backman bandwagon, but now that I'm on it I'm here to stay. I love *Beartown* for its depiction of small-town life and for its handling of a very tough topic with grace and empathy. In addition, the world of youth hockey is one I know almost nothing about, and Bachman managed to make the world both accessible and utterly enthralling at the same time. There is so much for a book club to discuss in these pages.

THE HATE U GIVE by Angie Thomas. I was so blown away by this book that after I finished it, I immediately wanted everyone I know to read it so we could discuss it. What more could you want out of a book club pick? Obviously, a lot of people have read it, but anyone who hasn't, needs to. It's rare for a young adult book to resonate equally with adults, and when that happens, people need to pay attention.

The way you make an omelet reveals your character.

—ANTHONY BOURDAIN

Cookbooks worth reading

- **Cook Korean! A Comic Book with Recipes** by Robin Ha
- **Prune** by Gabrielle Hamilton
- **The Smitten Kitchen Cookbook: Recipes and Wisdom from an Obsessive Home Cook** by Deb Perelman
- **From My Mother's Kitchen: Recipes and Reminiscences** by Mimi Sheraton
- **Heritage** by Sean Brock
- **A History of Food in 100 Recipes** by William Sitwell
- **My Two Souths: Blending the Flavors of India into a Southern Kitchen** by Asha Gomez
- **97 Orchards: An Edible History of Five Immigrant Families in One New York Tenement** by Jane Ziegelman
- **The Artists' and Writers' Cookbook** by Natalie Eve Garrett
- **Ripe: A Cook in the Orchard** by Nigel Slater
- **Tasting Rome: Fresh Flavors and Forgotten Recipes from an Ancient City** by Katie Parla and Kristina Gill
- **Dining In** by Alison Roman
- **Breakfast, Lunch, Dinner ... Life: Recipes and Adventures from My Home Kitchen** by Missy Robbins
- _____
- _____
- _____
- _____
- _____
- _____
- _____

Her Body and Other Parties:
Stories Carmen Maria Machado

A REDWALL-STYLE FEAST

WHAT TO EAT
WITH MY BOOK

Dijon and cognac beef stew, hot biscuits with honey butter, savory mushroom-cabbage hand pies, homemade pasta in homemade pesto, pelmeni (Russian dumplings) tossed in butter and vinegar, cocktail shrimp, and an assortment of cured meats, soft cheese, olives, and cornichons to nibble on. To drink: red wine, dirty martinis, Manhattans. Eat until you're content.

MY DREAM
DINNER TABLE
Women artists
who left us too
soon:
Shirley Jackson
Octavia Butler
Ana Mendieta
Laura Aguilar
Angela Carter

What to read next

FRESHWATER by Akwaeke Emezi

CONFESSIONS OF THE FOX by Jordy Rosenberg

A LUCKY MAN by Jamel Brinkley

LOST CHILDREN ARCHIVE by Valeria Luiselli

EVERYTHING UNDER by Daisy Johnson

Resistance Women
Jennifer Chiaverini

WHAT TO EAT WITH MY BOOK

MY DREAM DINNER TABLE Authors Margaret George and Mary Doria Russell because they're amazing, intelligent women who would bring wisdom, insight, and humor to the conversation. Jane Austen and Ada Lovelace, because I wish I could speak with them, and how else would I have the chance except in a hypothetical situation like this? I'd round out the party with my sister, Heather, because she's an avid reader and she'd love to meet Jane Austen.

JAEGERSCHNITZEL
(PORK LOIN WITH MUSHROOM GRAVY)

A delicious German meal would be the perfect setting for a book club discussion of *Resistance Women.* The menu could include *Jaegerschnitzel* (pork loin with mushroom gravy) accompanied by *Spaetzle* (egg noodles) and *Gurkensalat* (cucumber salad). Serve a favorite German wine or beer to drink and follow up with coffee and *Apfelkuchen* (apple cake) for dessert.

Jaegerschnitzel (Pork Loin with Mushroom Gravy)
From *The Quilter's Kitchen* by Jennifer Chiaverini

8 thin pork cutlets (just over 1 pound), pounded to ⅛-inch thickness

1 teaspoon kosher salt

½ teaspoon black pepper

2 large eggs, beaten

1½ cups panko bread crumbs

4 to 6 tablespoons vegetable oil

4 slices bacon, finely chopped

1 medium onion, finely chopped

1 pound button mushrooms, sliced

2 tablespoons unsalted butter

1 tablespoon all-purpose flour

2 cups chicken broth

2 tablespoons sour cream

1 teaspoon finely chopped fresh thyme

1 tablespoon finely chopped fresh parsley

1. Preheat the oven to 200°F. Have 2 plates lined with paper towels ready.

2. Sprinkle the pork cutlets with the salt and pepper.

3. Place the eggs in a shallow bowl. Place the bread crumbs on a plate.

4. Dip the cutlets in the beaten egg and then in the bread crumbs to coat evenly.

5. Place a large skillet over medium heat and when it is hot, add 2 tablespoons oil. Add the cutlets, in batches, and cook until evenly browned, about 3 minutes per side, adding oil as necessary. Place on the prepared plate to drain, then transfer to the oven to keep warm while you prepare the gravy.

6. Place the bacon in a large skillet over medium heat and cook until the fat is rendered and the bacon is crisp, 5 to 7 minutes. Remove the bacon with a slotted spoon to a paper-towel–lined plate to drain.

7. Raise the heat to high, add the onion, and cook until browned, 3 to 5 minutes. Add the mushrooms and butter and continue cooking until the mushrooms are soft and brown, about 10 additional minutes. Add the flour and stir to combine. Add the chicken broth and cook until reduced and thickened, about 5 minutes.

8. Remove from heat, add sour cream and herbs, and stir to combine. Serve immediately over the pork cutlets.

Serves 8.

ENCHANTRESS OF NUMBERS by Jennifer Chiaverini. My previous historical novel features Ada Byron King, Countess of Lovelace, the daughter of the renowned poet Lord Byron and an early 19th century mathematician who is credited with writing the first computer program long before the first computer was ever built.

A THREAD OF GRACE by Mary Doria Russell. Another tale of resistance, this inspiring, heartbreaking novel set in Italy during the last years of World War II tells the true story of ordinary Italian citizens who saved the lives of 43,000 Jews during the Nazi occupation.

STATION ELEVEN by Emily St. John Mandel. Her depiction of a global pandemic is harrowing, and the characters' experiences are brutal and utterly believable—and yet the novel is ultimately uplifting and redemptive.

Gulp: Adventures on the Alimentary Canal Mary Roach

**WHAT TO EAT
WITH MY BOOK**

**MY DREAM
DINNER TABLE**
The chance
to sit down to
a meal with
someone dead is
so extraordinary
that it hardly
matters who
it is. I have so
many questions:
What's a typical
day like? Do you
miss your body?
How are you
going to chew
these lamp
chops?

BEER AND PEANUTS

Start in the bar with a good beer and some peanuts. Exhale through your nose while holding the beer in your mouth. Sniffing on the exhale is called retronasal olfaction. You are experiencing the complex flavors of the beer through a second set of nostrils, in the back of your mouth. Don't overdo it on the exhaling, as this can lead to nasal regurgitation and snorted beer all over the book.

Now take a peanut between your upper and lower molars and bear down on it. As the peanut gives way, take a moment to appreciate the reflex that automatically registers the change in resistance and shuts off your jaw muscles. Without it, the pressure used to break the nut could also break your tooth.

For dinner, eat whatever you want, but you must pay close attention to what is happening to it inside your mouth. Bolus formation is what's happening. First your teeth grind up the food, and then your tongue, with help from your saliva, forms a rounded cylindrical mass that slides easily down your esophagus. Your tongue and teeth and saliva work tirelessly to get everything you eat into the swallowable state. This is a technical term that would also work well as the motto for Rhode Island.

What to read next

THE SISTERS BROTHERS by Patrick deWitt. I am presently devouring all of deWitt's books, barely pausing to digest one before scarfing another. *Under Majordomo Minor* and *French Exit* are also very tasty.

Notes

A Piece of the World
Christina Baker Kline

APPLE CAKE IN AN IRON SKILLET

MY DREAM
DINNER TABLE
I would of
course invite
Andrew Wyeth,
who painted
Christina for
30 years and
considered her
a close friend.
His wife, Betsy,
spent summers
at the Olson
house when she
was a child;
in fact, she
introduced Andy
to Christina
the very day
she met him
(Betsy and Andy
were married
10 months later;
she was only
17 years old.)
Christina's
brother Alvaro,
who lived with
her for his
entire life,
would also be
there, though
he wouldn't
talk much. And
it would be
thrilling for
Christina to
include Emily
Dickinson and
Willa Cather,
two of her
favorite writers.

Christina Olson, the real-life woman who was Andrew Wyeth's muse and is the subject of my novel, made three meals a day on a wood stove, an old black Glenwood range, in her rural Maine kitchen. I love getting photos from book clubs of dinners they've made that were inspired by Christina's cooking: haddock chowder; roasted chicken; Maine potatoes with hand-churned butter and herbs; new carrots; a platter of tomatoes sprinkled with salt; pickled fiddleheads, carrots, and cucumbers. For dessert? Christina was famous for her fried apple cake and gingerbread cookies.

My own fried apple cake recipe is a little light on specifics. I just followed Christina Olson's "add some flour, add some sugar" instructions. I found a great version—basically, the same thing —on the The Pioneer Woman website by Ree Drummond. This one is pretty much identical to Christina's except that it has measurements.

Apple Cake in an Iron Skillet

1 ¾ sticks butter

¾ cups sugar

4 or 5 whole Granny Smith apples, peeled, cored, and cut into 6 equal wedges

For the batter:

1 stick butter

⅔ cups sugar

1 ½ teaspoon vanilla

2 whole large eggs

½ cup sour cream

1 ½ cup all-purpose flour

1 ½ teaspoon baking powder

1 teaspoon salt

½ teaspoon cinnamon

1 whole small Granny Smith apple, peeled, cored, and chopped finely

Preheat oven to 375 F.

1. In a 9- to 10-inch skillet, melt 1 ¾ sticks butter over low heat. Add ¾ cup sugar to the pan and stir around, then place apple slices, cut side down, in the pan. Don't pack them too tightly, but try not to leave overly large gaps. Allow this to cook over low/medium-low heat while you make the cake batter.

2. In the bowl of an electric mixer, beat 1 stick of butter and ⅔ cup sugar until light and fluffy. Mix in vanilla and eggs. Add sour cream and mix well.

3. In a bowl, mix flour, baking powder, salt, and cinnamon. Stir together, then gradually add flour mixture into the creamed mixture until just combined. Gently stir in 1 chopped apple.

4. Remove skillet from heat. Spoon batter over the top, then spread gently so batter is evenly distributed. Bake for 20 to 25 minutes, or until cake is golden brown and bubbly. Allow cake to sit in skillet for 5 minutes, then invert onto a serving plate. Don't worry if some of the topping isn't perfect—it'll taste perfect!

Serve warm with vanilla ice cream.

From: thepioneerwoman.com/cooking/apple-cake-in-an-iron-skillet/

What to read next

If you liked reading about the characters in *A Piece of the World*, you might want to pick up my novel *Orphan Train*, which is also about rural people in the early to mid-20th century finding their way in the world. If the setting captivated you, try *The Way Life Should Be,* which takes place on an island off the coast of Maine.

Recent books by other authors I love include:

EDUCATED by Tara Westover

STATION ELEVEN by Emily St. John Mandel

THE UNDERGROUND RAILROAD by Colson Whitehead

PACHINKO by Min Jin Lee

First we eat, then we do everything else. —M.F.K. FISHER

Manhattan Beach Jennifer Egan

**WHAT TO EAT
WITH MY BOOK**

DEVILED CHICKEN

**MY DREAM
DINNER TABLE**
Winston
Churchill

Edith Wharton

William
Shakespeare

Barak and
Michelle Obama

Manhattan Beach mostly takes place during WWII, when meat was rationed and fruits and veggies were often canned. So I'm going to suggest Deviled Chicken.

Green beans, peas, or carrots (they would have been canned in the 1940s, but I'd do fresh)

Cherry Cobbler (my grandma's recipe—delicious!)

Deviled Chicken

1 broiling or frying chicken

salt and pepper

½ cup fat, melted

2 tbsp flour

1 cup hot water or soup stock

1 ½ tsp dry mustard

2 tsp Worcestershire sauce

2 tsp tomato ketchup

paprika

1. Allow ¾ lb chicken per person. Cut chicken into serving portions, season with salt and pepper, and brown in melted fat; remove from pan.

2. Stir flour into fat; cook until mixture browns and thickens, stirring constantly.

3. Add hot water or soup stock and next 4 ingredients to cooked sauce.

4. Place chicken in sauce, cover pan, and simmer until tender, about an hour.

From *250 Ways to Prepare Poultry and Game Birds*, edited by Ruth Berolzheimer, 1954

Cherry Cobbler Filling

2 1-lb cans of red tart cherries, drained

⅔ cup of sugar

2 tbsp cornstarch

1 cup juice from cherries

1 tbsp butter or margarine

¼ tsp cinnamon

Combine sugar and cornstarch. Add cherry juice and cook, stirring constantly until thick. Add cherries, butter, and cinnamon. Pour into an 8-inch square baking dish.

Cherry Cobbler Topping

1 cup sifted flour

2 tbsp sugar

2 tsp baking powder

½ tsp salt

½ cup milk (or so)

3 tbsp shortening

Sift dry ingredients together; cut in shortening. Add milk gradually and mix well with fork. Drop by tablespoons onto cherry mixture. Sprinkle sugar over pastry. Bake at 400 degrees for 30 minutes.

What to read next

THE HOUSE OF MIRTH by Edith Wharton

My favorite novel of all time. Smart, funny, crushing look at the addictive power of money and the scant opportunities that existed for a woman—even a beautiful one—in Gilded Age New York. A page-turner that will stay with you the rest of your life.

The Alice Network Kate Quinn

FRENCH AND ENGLISH CLASSICS FROM THE NOVEL

MY DREAM
DINNER TABLE
Elizabeth I the
Virgin Queen,
and Caterina
Sforza the Tiger
Countess-two
bad-ass women
of history I
admire hugely.

William
Shakespeare
and Leonardo
da Vinci-two
incredible minds
I'd love to pick.
And Oscar
Wilde, to keep
us all laughing.

This mix can be served in small portions as finger food or as a full, four-course meal.

Starters: Fried courgette flowers (zucchini blossoms), Duck rillettes with toast points

Soup: Lobster bisque

Main: Goat cheese and prosciutto sandwiches with frites

Dessert: Biscuits with clotted cream and rose jam

To Drink: Earl Grey tea, Provençal rosé

Delicious Drop Biscuits

1. Mix 4 cups flour, ¼ cup sugar, 2 tsp baking powder, 1 tsp salt, and ½ tsp baking soda in a mixing bowl.

2. Cube 2 sticks of ice-cold butter and add to the dry mixture. Cut in until mixture is crumbly.

3. Add 2 eggs to 1 cup buttermilk; whisk together briefly, then add to dry mixture and mix together with fork till moistened.

4. Turn dough out on floured surface, knead 5-6 times till it resembles a big scraggy lump. It will be messy, but only knead enough to pull the dough together; the less you handle it, the more tender the biscuits will be.

5. Pull off chunks into rough rounds, and space a few inches apart on greased baking sheet

6. Bake at 375 degrees until golden. (Baking time will depend on how big you like your biscuits.) Serve warm with clotted cream and rose jam, which can both be found online or at stores like Wegmans or Trader Joe's.

THE GUERNSEY LITERARY AND POTATO PEEL PIE SOCIETY by Annie Barrows and Mary Ann Shaffer. The best book about book clubs that every book club could ever hope to read! Pair with french fries, mashed potatoes, or your favorite potato dish rather than anything made with potato peelings.

SHINING THROUGH by Susan Isaacs. Best book ever about a female spy; you will cheer for the steely, courageous heroine as she enters World War II Berlin to work undercover as a cook for a high-ranking Nazi official. Pair with classic German dishes like the ones the heroine is constantly whipping up, from stuffed pheasant to meatballs in caper sauce.

THE HUNTRESS by Kate Quinn. My next book, all about the women who flew in the all-female night-bomber regiment nicknamed the Night Witches. Pair with Russian favorites like hot kasha with mushrooms, bright-red borscht with black bread, and ice-cold vodka.

Notes

Index

The most remarkable thing about my mother is that for 30 years she served the family nothing but leftovers. The original meal has never been found.

—CALVIN TRILLIN

First (and only) Edition

Printed in the United States of America
exclusively for Independent Bookstore Day 2019

Designer: Kristine Brogno
Editor: Samantha Schoech

ISBN 978-0-9984499-8-2

California Bookstore Day Publishing
A division of Independent Bookstore Day and
The Northern California Independent Booksellers Association
www.indiebookstoreday.com

CPSIA information can be obtained
at www.ICGtesting.com
Printed in the USA
LVHW052111210319
611477LV00003B/5/P